3 ¢

MW00778836

Fast-Start Guides for Entrepreneurs

FINANCE ESSENTIALS
FOR ENTREPRENEURS

*A Simple Guide to Understanding
and Creating Financial Statements
for Your Business*

NAEEM ZAFAR

Haas Business School,
University of California, Berkeley

www.Startup-Advisor.com

Finance Essentials for Entrepreneurs:
A Simple Guide to Understanding and Creating Financial Statements for Your Business

Copyright © 2010 by Naeem Zafar.

Published by:

Five Mountain Press

Five Mountain Press
Cupertino, California USA
info@FiveMountainPress.com
www.FiveMountainPress.com

ISBN 13: 978-0-9823420-7-7
ISBN 10: 0-9823420-7-1
Printed in the United States of America

I am grateful to the many CFOs and other knowledgeable professionals who took the time to review this eBook and provided valuable input.

I am especially grateful to Jack Fuchs, Bob Bylin, and Betty Kayton (all of whom have served as Chief Financial Officers for private and public companies) for their time and consideration in helping to clean up many versions of my manuscript.

TABLE OF CONTENTS

Chapter 1

WHY DO I NEED TO LEARN
ABOUT FINANCE?

Most entrepreneurs are not financial wizards. Often, they have never worked with any financial statements. They may never even have looked at a financial statement! But if they want to run a business, they must be comfortable with the financial aspects of their endeavor.

Entrepreneurs do not need to be financial experts. At some point, however, they will need to hire a financial expert who can take care of that part of their business. That being said, entrepreneurs <u>do</u> need some rudimentary understanding of finances. This eBook provides just enough information for entrepreneurs to understand financial statements, assumptions, and projections. It is intended to make a new entrepreneur feel that he or she has a handle on how a company can (and should) operate.

In order for an entrepreneur to gain investor confidence and receive funding, he or she must create a very basic financial model for his or her business. I will help you create that model in this short eBook. Keep in mind that this is business finance *simplified*! Some CFOs (Chief Financial Officers) may cringe at how simplified the information is. But what I'm giving you in this book is just enough—the bare minimum of the financial information that you need to master in order to be a successful entrepreneur. Don't worry. I will make it easy.

This eBook will offer you "what-if" scenarios and help you understand what drives the business. It will also show what assumptions you must track (and see actually happen) in order to have a successful business. This may sound complicated, but in reality it isn't rocket science. I will walk you through the whole process.

I must admit that I have never taken a formal finance course. The topic never interested me. But I had to learn quickly about finance when I became the CEO of a startup. After that, I helped other startups with their business plans. My knowledge of startup finances comes from real-world, hands-on experience.

My explanation of financial terms and practices skips the arcane details and the theory. Instead, I focus on explaining what an entrepreneur needs to know in order to start a company, successfully write a business plan, and run the company with the proper financial controls in place.

I explain all of it in this simple eBook.

What Are the Most Important Documents?

There are three documents with which you will need to become familiar: The income statement, the balance sheet, and the cash flow statement. Cash is your oxygen. It is very difficult to run a business without understanding cash flow. It is vital, but it is not complex. The cash flow statement shows you how cash is coming in and going out.

You will, however, spend most of your time with the income statement, which shows your revenue assumptions, your expense projections, and your anticipated profits. I will explain how to build this statement shortly.

One big reason for learning financial fundamentals is to gain clarity about your business. The main thing you need to be clear about is whether the business makes sense in the first place. You are about to make a huge sacrifice to start a company. It is going to take a toll on your savings. It will definitely affect your relationships. It may even affect your health! At the very least, it will probably impact several years of your life. It is unwise to start this journey without first considering whether the business idea makes financial sense.

In order to get that kind of clarity, you will need to make a list of financial assumptions and run a few scenarios.

You will also need to have a rudimentary grasp of finances in order to convince your investors that their money will be safe with you. No sane investor is going to give you his or her hard-earned money unless you can demonstrate that you are competent to manage that money and make money for him or her. This means being comfortable with financial projections and financial assumptions, and being able to defend your financial plans.

Fortunately, using this book and the many other tools available to you will enable you to accomplish these things. I will show you that grasping the basics of finance is much easier than you may have imagined. With very little information, you can master all the financial know-how you need to succeed as an entrepreneur.

Chapter 2

FINANCIAL ASSUMPTIONS

The most important component of understanding your business is your cash flow statement. A cash flow statement will tell how much cash you need and what to do with it when you get it. The cash flow statement will also allow you to answer several key questions about your business. A cash flow statement helps you achieve clarity by letting you examine some key financial assumptions and giving you a way to measure and validate them.

Start by looking at what financial assumptions you are making about your business. Every type of business is driven by a handful of primary financial assumptions. As long as you know what they are and you have a way of validating them, you are in good shape.

The best way to come up with these financial assumptions is by looking at examples from other businesses. Once you define the assumptions in terms of your business, the rest of the plan can be built on those financial assumptions. Sometimes the assumptions are represented as key performance indicators, or KPIs.

Most investors understand that it is difficult to accurately project your revenue over three to five years. That being said, investors *do* want to know about your thought process in creating those projections. In other words, how did you come to the projections you are presenting to them? Investors are more likely to trust the integrity of your projections if you are able to defend your financial assumptions. For example, they want to know which key performance indicators you watched, as well as see comparisons to other companies in your industry. They will want to know whether the growth rate or rationale you have derived is legitimate, based on the examples of the other businesses you have looked at.

So, in addition to your financial assumptions, you should have a strategy for validating those assumptions. This validation can come from your own research, looking at publicly available data from other companies, and your own initial execution of the company plans.

What You Must Know

I would like you to have these three answers on the tip of your tongue when you are ready to meet with and pitch to investors. (These are good questions to answer for yourself, even if you are not raising funds.)

1) How much cash do you need to get to the break-even point?

2) How many months will it be before you get to the break-even point?

3) What will your run rate be (per month or per quarter) when you reach this break-even point?

Remember that the break-even point is when your expenses equal your revenue for a given period (perhaps monthly; usually quarterly). When you are able to stand up and confidently give the following answers to those questions—$850,000, 17 months, $280K per quarter— then the listener knows that you have done your homework. (Of course, these are just examples. You will need to calculate your own answers after doing the exercises in this eBook.)

STARTING A RESTAURANT

Let's take a simple example: starting a restaurant. What key assumptions will drive your business? Of course, there are startup costs: buying equipment, securing a lease, and hiring people. There will also be the recurring costs of running the business.

One of the things I would worry about is how profitable the operations will be. In order to have an idea of whether this restaurant can be profitable, I will make the following three assumptions:

1) Each table will spend, on average, $45 per seating;

2) An average of 70% of the tables will be filled per week;

3) Each table will turn over three times per night (a 6:30 p.m. seating, an 8 p.m. seating, and then a 9:30 p.m. seating).

It might be possible to make several other assumptions, but for the sake of simplicity we must always use the two, three, or four most relevant assumptions. Do as much research as possible to make sure these assumptions are correct. Be willing to take corrective action if they are not.

Based on these simple assumptions, I am now able to construct a financial statement. (We will walk through the process in the next chapter.) We can analyze the financial operation of the business by watching these three indicators like gauges on a dashboard.

If we see, for example, that the average amount spent per table is less than $45, we can adjust our scenario accordingly. The following corrective actions may make sense:

- Change the menu and add additional appetizers, more expensive beverages, or desserts;

- Look at overall profitability and see if you can still make money with a lower per-table spending amount;

- Change some other assumptions, such as turning the tables a fourth time per night so that your profit per table comes out higher, even with lower spending.

Let's assume that you do get $45 per table in spending, and that your cost of delivering food is $32. This results in a net profit per table seating of $13. Turning a table three times a night results in a profit of $13 x 3 = $39 per table per night.

You may also notice that you are turning the tables only twice a night. This means that instead of making $39 in profit per table per night, you are now making only $13 x 2 = $26 per night. What will you do now? Again, you have a number of options:

- Raise pricing or offer more expensive items, so that even by turning a table just twice a night your profit will increase per table per night.

- Change the music in the restaurant to a slightly faster beat. This has been shown to make people eat faster, which may result in turning tables three times per night.

- Hire speedier waiters and streamline kitchen operations so that you can reduce the total time (on average) per table.

- Implement some form of cost reduction. For example, you could reduce portion sizes, negotiate better prices with suppliers, or substitute cheaper ingredients in the recipes.

As you can see, there are a few ways in which you can arrange the variables in this business with an eye to the total profit per table or per night. Once you have built the right financial model, you can play with these assumptions and create what-if scenarios that will help your business achieve your financial goals.

HOW DO I PICK THE RIGHT NUMBERS?

An entrepreneur should do this as simply as possible. Getting a handle on the numbers does not require an MBA or a lot of expensive market research. I would watch other restaurants in the area to see how often they are turning tables per night. I would ask the waiter smoking in the back alley about how much people spend per table. A few of these data points can help me understand the basic dynamics of the business. I would even watch a given restaurant each night for a month to determine how many tables were occupied and what the spending and traffic patterns were.

These are not scientific ways to gather solid data. But they do provide the kind of basic first-order data that an entrepreneur needs. I can track these indicators on my own KPI dashboard and monitor them in my own place in order to see what the actual numbers are. If need be, I can modify and correct my assumptions.

Each business runs on a few basic assumptions. Even large electronics or technology firms have a relatively small set of assumptions they use in projections. You can use this model for businesses of every size, no matter what industry your business is in.

Other examples: You are a consultant. Your assumptions would revolve around the percentage of billable hours compared to total hours. Or, you run a factory that makes semiconductor chips. You run your assumptions based on the percentage of capacity filled and yield (meaning, what percentage of chips started are actually completed and functional after the processing steps are completed). The restaurant example is not as simplistic as you may think. Every business runs on a few key assumptions.

WHY FINANCIAL ASSUMPTIONS MATTER

Investors know that anyone can be an Excel jockey and manipulate numbers to make them come out right for you. What they really care about are your financial assumptions. You must know what your key assumptions are—and you must be able to explain how you have validated them. Each business will have different assumptions that are suitable for their business plan. Examples of such assumptions include:

a) Customer acquisition cost

b) The cost of manufacturing one unit

c) Monthly subscription revenues

d) The CPM you think you can command (the cost per thousand impressions that your internet ad earns)

e) Profit per customer visit

Your choice of assumptions, and how you validate them, shows how much insight you really have into your business.

Example:

Let's say you are expecting a $3 per-customer acquisition cost. You choose to advertise your business through Google AdWords. You choose 80 cents ($0.80) as the maximum amount you are willing to pay when people click on your ad. But you find out after a few days of testing that for every ten people that click on your ad, only one completes the transaction. This brings your customer acquisition cost to eight dollars per customer ($0.80 x 10 = $8)!

With an actual acquisition cost of $8 per customer, your initial assumption of a $3 per-customer acquisition cost is completely out of whack. You can:

a) Redo your financial projections using $8 as the new assumption for customer acquisition cost;

b) Change your landing page content so that one out of every four people clicks to become a customer (1:4 at $0.80 means a $3.20 per-customer acquisition cost) or

c) Reduce your Google ad bid price to \$0.30 so that a 10:1 conversion yields a \$3 customer acquisition cost.

Your chosen tactic will depend on many factors. My hope is that you can see the value in knowing, validating, and keeping an eye on your key financial assumptions.

Chapter 3

TYPES OF
FINANCIAL STATEMENTS

To raise money and convince yourself of the success of your business plan, you need a profit and loss (P&L) statement, as well as a cash flow statement and a balance sheet. (Actually, a balance sheet is not very relevant when you are just starting out and have almost no assets. My hope is that you will need one in the near future!)

You will need to build an income statement first. The other statements will then be extracted from it. As an entrepreneur, you can build a basic P&L statement; then your CFO or finance expert will add the additional data, such as timing of vendor payments, timing of customer collections, depreciation, amortization, and taxes.

REVENUE RECOGNITION

Even if you have collected money from a customer, it may not all be recognized as income on the income statement. Let us say, for example, that a customer pays you $10,000 for customer support and bug fixes for the next year. You have the money in your bank, but on your income statement, $1/12^{th}$ of that amount will show up every month as "recognized" income (the $10,000 will be recognized as income only as the service is rendered). This is an example of how your finance expert or CFO can come in and add the additional information using proper accounting principles. The specifics of when you can recognize revenue are complex and best left to a finance expert. I am illustrating this point here only to indicate that there is a difference between the actual cash collected and the income recognized on your income statement.

WHY IS THE CASH FLOW STATEMENT IMPORTANT?

To an entrepreneur, cash is king. You may be able to "book" an order after having sold the product. It shows up as income, but you may not see the cash for 60 days. Your income statement indicates that you have income, but you do not have the cash. Cash is the factor that drives commerce and your business.

Consider this: If you buy an $18,000 piece of machinery, your income statement will show this as $500 of depreciation expense for each of the next 36 months (using a concept called depreciation, which spreads the expense of this machinery over its three-year useful life). But even though the P&L only shows a $500 per-month expense, in reality you spent $18,000 up front to buy this machinery, and in reality $18,000 left your pocket last week. That hurts! And only your cash flow statement shows the hurt. It indicates how the cash is entering or leaving the business.

In other words, although you may have bought some machinery that is depreciating by so much per month over a 36-month period, the fact is that the cash left your company when you bought the machinery. A cash flow statement shows that the money used to purchase the machinery left your business during a certain month. Your P&L statement will not show that. The P&L will show your initial expenses in starting the business (acquisition of a patent or technology, for example) as being amortized over several months, and capital equipment purchases as being depreciated over many years.

THE INCOME STATEMENT

This is the most common statement you will use. It will be in your investor presentation and form a part of your business plan. It shows the sources of your revenue, the sources of your expenses, and your assumptions of gross and net profit. It helps people understand how much money you will make and how much cash you will need before you start generating profits.

My suggestion is that you start by doing a monthly financial statement until your business becomes profitable. After that, you can do them quarterly; then, in a few years, perhaps annually. I suggest doing a monthly analysis for the first twenty-four months. After twenty-four months, go to quarterly statements for one or two years. For the two years after that, do annual statements. You need to have approximately a five- or six-year window to do your projections, but for the most part the effort will go into the first two years. I am going to walk you through the process of creating such statements in a way that is easy to understand.

STATEMENT OF CASH FLOW (SCF)

Definition: A statement of cash flow (SCF) is designed to show how the firm's operations have affected its cash position. It does this by examining how the firm has used its cash in terms of its investment and financing decisions.

Income Statement vs. Cash Flow Statement

Income Statement

Net Sales (revenue)

– COS (cost of sales)

= Gross Profit

– Fixed operating costs {Salaries, etc.} (except depreciation)

= EBITDA
(earnings before interest, taxes, depreciation, & amortization)

– Depreciation and amortization

= Net Operating Income (NOI) = EBIT

– Interest

= EBT

– Taxes

= Net Income

Also, for simplicity,
Net Income + Depreciation and Amortization = Net Cash Flow from Operations (or Net Profit)

P&L shows cash gain or loss from operations, but you also have to consider the changes in working capital to get to full cash flow. That will be reflected in the Balance Sheet.

A true SCF starts with net income and adjusts it for additions and subtractions as defined above to arrive at net cash flow from operations. To this we can add or subtract cash flow (CF) from investment activities and CF from financing activities to arrive at the net change in cash.

Chapter 4

ANATOMY OF A P&L OR INCOME STATEMENT

THE BALANCE SHEET

The balance sheet is important because it shows the liabilities that must be covered and the deployment of the opening cash into the various assets required to support the enterprise. You cannot leave this financial perspective out. No doubt about it, cash is king and cash flow is important to understand—but you have to have a valid balance sheet for two periods in order to create a credible cash flow for the period in between.

What you will be presenting in your business plan (and investor pitch) is a single Excel spreadsheet that contains roughly a dozen rows and half a dozen columns. It will show the following data points: revenue, cost of sales (COS), gross profit, expenses, and net profit (before complicating life with taxes, amortization, depreciation, and interest). I will explain all of these terms below. Here is an example of what such a statement will look like:

Income Statement

	2009	2010	2011	2012	2013
Revenues	-	750,000	3,600,000	8,450,000	29,250,000
Costs of sales		225,000	900,000	2,112,500	7,312,500
Gross Profit	-	525,000	2,700,000	6,337,500	21,937,500
Research and development	840,000	960,000	1,200,000	1,400,000	3,200,000
Technology payment	300,000	-	-	-	-
Sales and marketing	-	920,000	1,760,000	2,878,000	8,688,000
General and admin	620,000	660,000	1,100,000	1,600,000	2,300,000
Total operating expenses	1,760,000	2,540,000	4,060,000	5,878,000	14,188,000
Net income (loss) from operations	(1,760,000)	(2,015,000)	(1,360,000)	459,500	7,749,500
Other income (expense)	200,000	300,000	420,000	100,000	50,000
Net income (loss) before taxes	(1,560,000)	(1,715,000)	(940,000)	559,500	7,799,500
Taxes	-	-		139,875	1,949,875
Net income (loss)	(1,560,000)	(1,715,000)	(940,000)	699,375	9,749,375

Notes:

1) Cost of Sales (COS) is often used interchange-ably with the term Cost of Goods Sold (COGS). I use COS as a more generic term, since many businesses do not sell any actual goods (Software-as-a-service or information products are often downloads or used on the website as a subscription).

2) I have shown a one-time technology payment to illustrate that you may have some special payments or expenses best shown separately so that others can note the event rather than as-

sume that your numbers are unusually high in any one department.

3) In this example, general and administrative (G&A) expenses are rather high. There may be some special considerations relevant to this particular spreadsheet. For example, this company had setups in three countries from the start, which creates high G&A expenses. These types of issues should be explained in a footnote.

Perhaps surprisingly, this simple statement reveals a lot. It will show the following pieces of data:

- The revenue growth expectations and rates;

- The expense growth rate;

- The amount of money this company will require before turning a profit; and

- The inherent profitability of this business (as compared to other businesses an investor might put his or her money in).

But let's define some of these terms first:

Term	Explanation
Revenue	This is the actual revenue booked according to Generally Accepted Accounting Principles (GAAPs) due to complicated rules about revenue recognition. In simple businesses and in a cash flow statement, this will be the actual cash collected. This is what an entrepreneur really cares about (you should let your accountant or CFO deal with actual GAAP-compliant revenue calculations).
COS	Cost of Sales is the actual cost of delivering your product or service on a per-unit basis after the first unit is created. In other words, the cost of creating the first unit may be very high because of the research and development needed. But after that money has been spent, you must calculate how much each unit costs you, then multiply it by the number of units sold. For example, if you make dolls, then the COS will be found by adding up the costs of the materials and labor for each doll, the average cost per doll of running (not building) the factory, and the average cost per doll of running the call center that sells the dolls. You would then take that amount and multiply it by the number of dolls sold to determine the COS. For software businesses, the COS can be negligible (possibly just the cost of a CD or servers and hosting to enable product downloads).

Term	Explanation
Gross Profit	Subtracting the COS from revenue will give you your Gross Profit. This is the profit before you subtract any expenses for running the business. It is important to note that unless you have a healthy gross profit it will be impossible to have a healthy net income. This number can be as high as over 90% for software businesses. It is typically 60% or so for high-tech hardware businesses, and may be as low as 10% to 20% for service-oriented businesses.
SG&A	Sales, General, and Administrative costs include all sales, marketing, and administrative costs. Normally I like to see this broken down according to department in a P&L statement. This is why in the example above I show R&D (Research and Development), S&M (Sales and Marketing), and G&A (General and Administrative) expenses on separate lines. This reveals a lot more than combining them in one single SG&A line.
Opex	Operating Expenses—these are often the same as research and development expenses plus SG&A. These are the recurring costs of running a business.

Term	Explanation
Capex	Capital Expenses: These apply when you are buying expensive items such as machinery or computers that can be depreciated according to the tax laws—not every business will have Capex.
Net Income	Subtracting SG&A from Gross Profit gives us the EBITDA (see definition below). Once we subtract depreciation & amortization, we have the NOI (Net Operating Income) or EBIT (Earnings Before Interest and Taxes). Net Income is derived by then deducting interest and taxes.
EBITDA	(Often pronounced EE-Bit-Dah.) This acronym stands for Earnings Before Interest, Taxes, Depreciation, & Amortization. For a startup, this is often the business's income, as the other portions are not likely to be significant for you. EBITDA is your income for all practical purposes. If this amount is negative, then you will have to raise the amount you lack from other sources (investors) to make it through.

GROSS MARGIN

The gross margin is a very important thing for an entrepreneur to keep his or her eye on. It tells you and an investor if there is enough money per transaction to make the company interesting. If you are selling dollar bills for 98 cents, you may have huge revenues, but you will be losing money no matter how efficiently you run the company. (Such a practice will result in a negative gross margin, by the way.) You want healthy and positive gross margins!

Each industry has a standard expectation for the gross margin. The formula is

$$GM = (Price - Cost)/Price$$
expressed as a percentage.

If the price of a widget is $80 and the cost is $20, then the gross margin will be 75%. If the cost is $40, then the gross margin will be 50%.

If you have a company in the software industry, a gross margin of 35% will raise immediate suspicion in a business plan reader (especially an investor, since their eyes are trained to go look for these issues like a laser beam!). The software industry enjoys gross margins of 80% or higher, while a systems company can demonstrate margins ranging from 30% to 60%. The PC industry is so price-competitive that they often work on single-digit gross margins. Grocery stores and other industries that can turn their inventory over several times a month can work on even lower gross margins, since they turn over their inventory several times a year.

The following example helped clarify this concept for me. Let us say that a street hawker has a cost of $40 for his goods and he works on a gross margin of 50%. His expectation is to sell all the goods (fruit, for example) by the end of the day. So he aims for total sales per day of $80. This gives him a simple gross margin of 50%. This also means that his gross profit is $40 per day. But what if he changes his location or obtains a bicycle and can cover more ground per day? Perhaps he can sell all his goods by midday. Then he can buy more fruit and will be able to sell his fruit by the end of the day in a different neighborhood. Now he has turned the inventory twice per day. He can perhaps make $80 in a single day ($40 on the first basket, then buying more fruit and making another $40 on the second basket). His gross margin is still 50%, but by turning the inventory twice in a day he doubles his gross profit.

This offers some exciting options for this street hawker. He can be more competitive by lowering his gross margin to a lower number (e.g., 30%) and still eke out more dollars in gross profit in his pocket. If he is able to move more inventory by serving two neighborhoods in one day (due to his investment in the bicycle), he can look at other ways to improve his inventory turnover. Perhaps he can rent a motorcycle and turn his inventory over more than twice a day. Or perhaps he can invest in a bigger display or bigger basket so that even at the fixed gross margin he can improve his gross profit.

Chapter 5

HOW TO CONSTRUCT A P&L STATEMENT IN THREE EASY SECTIONS

The fact is that the P&L (Profit and Loss) statement you need to create on an Excel spreadsheet is really not that complex. It has three basic sections. Section 1 is Revenue, Section 2 is Expenses, and Section 3 is Net Profits. Once you have those sections filled out, you can do some simple ratios for a sanity check.

A P&L statement is very important because it provides you with clarity and insight into what makes a business work (or not).

How does one build such a P&L statement? In simple terms, you build the expense side and the revenue side separately, and then combine them to create net income. Let's look at each section individually to see what each should contain.

SECTION 1:
BUILDING THE REVENUE EQUATION

Start by simply listing your main sources of revenue. The revenue can be from any source: a single product, multiple products, and/or different divisions of your business. Let's look at some examples:

For an Internet-based business, sources of revenue may include one or more of the following:

- Subscription revenue;
- Advertising revenue;
- Product sales or licenses.

If you were selling a device or a piece of software, the revenue sources might include device or software sales and service maintenance. Typically, companies pay maintenance fees of 15% to 20% of the software price per year in order to receive minor upgrades or bug fixes. In consumer software, the pricing model is either a one-time charge (think of sales for a product such as Microsoft Office) or a monthly or yearly subscription (think of antivirus software companies).

It may be tempting to oversimplify and combine all your revenues into one line. But I suggest that you break the revenue sources into different categories. This will enable you to gain insights into the workings of your business. One possibility is to separate different sources into separate rows and group products by their different profit margins (such as hardware and software).

Your revenue picture may look something like this. (Note: Right-justify headings to improve readability. You'll also want to format the chart to make Row 4*5 = Row 6, add lines to show where the totals occur, make it clear that Line 4 is the number of subscribers (not $), and so on.)

Revenue	January	February	March	April	May	June	July
Number of Subscriptions	0	10	80	180	400	750	1250
Price per subscriber	$ 3	$ 3	$ 3	$ 3	$ 3	$ 3	$ 3
Total subscription revenue	$ -	$ 30	$ 240	$ 540	$ 1,200	$ 2,250	$ 3,750
Ad revenue	$ -	$ -	$ -	$ -	$ -	$ 500	$ 800
Total revenue	$ -	$ 30	$ 240	$ 540	$ 1,200	$ 2,750	$ 4,550

For the next example, let's assume that your revenue is derived from selling widgets. Take the number of widgets sold per month (or the number you expect to sell) and the price of each widget. Multiply the two together. This number yields your revenue projections.

Keep in mind that a company (such as this widget maker) may have other sources of revenue, which may include:

- Advertising;
- Subscriptions;
- Sales of multiple products.

While trying to construct these revenue projections, you may want to list each source of revenue in a separate line. Once you provide some details, add these lines together, and they will give you your total revenue.

Let's see how this works in the example of the widget maker. Start by listing the number of widgets that you will sell per month and the Average Selling Price (ASP) for each month. (Another approach is to start with the list price and use a row of typical discounts to compute the ASP in the third row.) Indicate COS and other items such as sales commissions, affiliate fees, shipping if significant, and the like.

So your quarterly revenues may look like this:

Revenue	1Q	2Q	3Q	4Q	5Q	6Q	7Q
Product revenue	$ 10.00	$ 12.00	$ 15.00	$ 18.00	$ 24.00	$ 28.00	$ 36.00
services	$ 2.00	$ 2.40	$ 3.00	$ 3.60	$ 4.80	$ 5.60	$ 7.20
IP licensing	$ 1.50	$ 1.50	$ 1.50	$ 1.50	$ 7.50	$ 7.50	$ 7.50
Total Revenue	$ 13.50	$ 15.90	$ 19.50	$ 23.10	$ 36.30	$ 41.10	$ 50.70
COS (Cost of Sales)	$ 6.00	$ 7.20	$ 9.00	$ 10.80	$ 14.40	$ 16.80	$ 21.60
Gross Profit	$ 7.50	$ 8.70	$ 10.50	$ 12.30	$ 21.90	$ 24.30	$ 29.10

In this example, revenue per quarter consists of three sources of revenue that help us understand the dynamics of the business. There is a more complex spreadsheet that helps us arrive at these numbers (e.g., sources of COS).

In order to support the findings in this report, you will have to compute the details of how you arrived at these numbers. Also, you will need to be clear about the proxies you considered before choosing the growth rates on a monthly or quarterly basis. This is described in my book on market research (www.FiveMountainPress.com). These details will only be shown in the business plan; they will not appear in your investor presentation. In the business plan, you must give more details about how the numbers were computed and provide some basis or data for your assumptions (proxy, actual data, projections, and the like).

After you have outlined your sources of revenue, the next thing to subtract from the revenue is your Cost of Goods Sold (COGS) or its more generic version, Cost of Sales (COS)—the direct cost of selling each unit of whatever you sell. (In the widget example, the cost of making the piece, plus the variable cost of selling that piece, is your COS). Variable cost includes shipping packaging (and possibly any royalties that you have to pay per widget) and all costs associated with the ability to sell that widget. It does NOT include your fixed selling costs, such as the salaries of salespeople and marketing campaigns. These fixed costs are there whether you sell 1 or 100 widgets in a month. These fixed costs are reflected in SG&A or OPEX numbers. The variable costs are included in COS.

Suppose that in one month you sold 100 widgets at $100 each, which means widget sales totaled $10,000. But the cost of the widget, let's say, is $30 dollars each.

Your total cost of goods sold is $30 * 100 = $3,000. That doesn't include shipping costs, plus any cost of assembling that widget or packaging it, or any of the incremental costs of supporting it.

What About Support Cost?

Suppose you have a call center that deals with supporting customers for this widget. It costs you $2,000 a month. This means that for every 100 widgets sold, your support cost is $20 per widget, in addition to the manufacturing costs and shipping costs.

If this is a fixed cost—meaning that it costs you $2,000 per month whether you sell one widget or many—it should be added to your expenses in section 2. If this is a variable cost, then we should add it to COS and subtract on a per-widget basis. If a company charges you $2 per call to handle support and the cost changes based on how many calls they took, then it makes sense to add this $2 per call to the COS.

UNDERSTANDING UNIT ECONOMICS

You really must be clear on the cost and revenue per additional unit that you sell. Are you selling dollar bills for 98 cents? The unit economics is the concept that should provide this clarity.

The Cost of Sale (COS) deals with the costs *directly associated with producing that one widget* (or possibly a service required for generating the revenue from that widget). In reality, what matters isn't that the cost is fixed or variable. The determining factor is whether the cost is actually associated with delivering the unit.

The costs of research and development, as well as marketing and sales, are not included in the COS. Accounting rules classify these expenses as "operating expenses," not as COS. But direct costs associated with making the product or service you are selling should be part of the cost of sales. Subtracting this number from your total revenue yields the gross profit. Gross profit is the last line in the revenue section.

Revenue	Q1	Q2	Q3	Q4	Year 1	Year 2	Year 3	Year 4	Year 5
Number of systems	0	2	2	3	7	22	47	97	186
Average selling price (ASP)	$250	$250	$250	$250	$250	$250	$350	$350	$350
Maintenance & Service	$0	$0	$20	$20	$40	$70	$220	$470	$970
Total Revenue	$ -	$ 500	$ 520	$ 770	$ 1,790	$ 5,570	$ 16,670	$ 34,420	$ 66,070
Average cost per system	$70	$70	$70	$70	$70	$66	$64	$64	$61
Total system cost	$0	$140	$140	$210	$490	$1,452	$3,008	$6,206	$11,346
Affiliate fee & commission	$0	$ 54	$ 54	$ 81	$ 189	$ 594	$ 1,269	$ 2,619	$ 5,022
shipping	$ -	$ 8	$ 8	$ 12	$ 28	$ 88	$ 188	$ 388	$ 744
COS	$70	$272	$272	$373	$777	$2,200	$4,529	$9,279	$17,173
Gross Profit	$ -	$ 228	$ 248	$ 397	$ 1,013	$ 3,370	$ 12,141	$ 25,141	$ 48,897

This detail is necessary for you and your business plan, but you only need to include certain parts of this report in your investor presentation. Feel free to hide certain columns and rows in Excel. In your investor presentation, the report may look like this:

Revenue					
	Year 1	Year 2	Year 3	Year 4	Year 5
Total Revenue	$ 1,790	$ 5,570	$ 16,670	$ 34,420	$ 66,070
COS	$777	$2,200	$4,529	$9,279	$17,173
Gross Profit	$ 1,013	$ 3,370	$ 12,141	$ 25,141	$ 48,897

Keep in mind, of course, that for your business the rows in the P&L and Revenue spreadsheets will probably have different titles than the ones I have used above. Your titles may include monthly subscriptions, or expected ad revenues, or some other metric that measures the number of events, transactions, or systems sold.

SECTION 2: EXPENSES

Now we are ready to look at the expense side of things. Usually you should start with the employee headcount. You need to figure out how many people we need and make an average estimate of their salaries. You will also add a few additional items if applicable:

1) You may use a standard number for rent, office expenses, travel, etc. on a fixed-dollar-amount-per-person basis (e.g., $800 per person per month for management or sales people and $300 per person per month for everyone else). You may also choose to itemize these costs separately if the situation demands it. Normally, fixed costs (such as rent, utilities, office expenses, Internet, etc.) are best tabulated separately under G&A expenses. That will usually yield a more accurate picture of your expenses.

2) You may consider using a round figure of 22% to 25% fringe expenses on top of the salaries to account for payroll taxes, medical benefits, and other administrative expenses. This number is appropriate to use in the USA. In other coun-

tries, you will need to calculate or estimate these numbers for yourself.

You can list these items separately, but initially it is fine to use such a multiplier for the overall payroll per month. (Figure the overhead this way: payroll taxes, 8.5%; medical expenses, 8% to 12%; and the rest covers the miscellaneous office expenses listed as fixed costs in #1 above.)

This way of approximating costs is usually sufficient for a high-tech entrepreneur. If you are opening a shop or have inventories, then you may need to list the fixed costs separately and properly so that it is more accurate.

3) Add any big, special items unique to your business such as:

   a. Technology license fees, if applicable;

   b. IT or web hosting costs (if large; otherwise it can be a small percentage added onto each employee in #1 above);

c. Special marketing expenses, if applicable (e.g., you must do two large trade shows per year, or you plan to launch a big ad campaign in October).

d. Any other major expense. For example, the rental or leasing of equipment can be a significant item if you have a non-IT business.

Then you can add additional special expenses and break it down by department. There will typically be four or five categories in this section. The four or five categories could be:

1) General administrative expenses;

2) Research and development expenses;

3) Marketing and sales expenses;

4) Any significant other expenses (which may be itemized if you have some expensive equipment or requirement that you have to purchase, or any one-time payments for marketing campaigns). If you were to buy capital equipment, that will show up in the balance sheet and cash

flow and a suitable notation will be made in the income statement.

Inside each of these rows you will need to show a detailed breakdown of where the expenses are coming from.

My suggestion is that you start by listing what kind of people you need in each of these departments and when. I usually start by making twenty-four-month charts and indicating the type of person needed. For example, we need one software person in month two, expanding to three in month six, and growing to eight in month eleven. Then you can assume an average salary for such a position. Multiply these, and you get your total value of salary expenses.

The result may look something like this:

Headcount and Salary Expenses

	Annual Salary	1/2010	2/2010	3/2011	4/2010	5/2010	6/2010	7/2010	8/2010	9/2010	10/2010	11/2010	12/2010
Administration													
CEO	$120,000	1	1	1	1	1	1	1	1	1	1	1	1
COO	120,000								1	1	1	1	1
CFO	120,000									1	1	1	1
Admin Assistant	30,000	1	1	1	1	1	1	1	1	1	1	1	1
Office Mgr	60,000							1	1	1	1	1	1
Administration Headcount		2	2	2	2	2	2	3	4	5	5	5	5
Engineering													
VP Engineering	$120,000	1	1	1	1	1	1	1	1	1	1	1	1
Lead Software engineer	110,000	1	1	1	1	1	1	1	1	1	1	1	1
Developers	90,000	1	4	6	8	8	8	8	9	9	9	9	9
Sys Admin	75,000	1	1	1	1	1	1	1	1	1	1	1	1
QA	75,000					1	2	2	2	2	2	2	2
UI	80,000					1	2	2	2	2	2	2	2
Engineering Headcount		4	7	9	11	13	15	15	16	16	16	16	16
Operations													
Webmaster	75,000							1	1	1	1	1	1
Tech Writer	84,000										1	1	1
Tech Support 1	75,000											2	3
Training Consultant	60,000												1
Implementation Consultant	86,000												1
Operations Headcount		0	0	0	0	0	0	1	1	1	2	4	7
Marketing & Sales													
VP Marketing	$120,000	1	1	1	1	1	1	1	1	1	1	1	1
VP Sales	120,000							1	1	1	1	1	1
Marketing Assistant	45,000										1	1	1
Account Exec	80,000											1	1
Product Mgr	90,000							1	1	1	1	1	1
Marketing & Sales Headcount		1	1	1	1	1	1	3	3	3	4	5	5
Total Headcount		7	10	12	14	16	18	22	24	25	27	30	33

You do have some flexibility here. Some of these people (such as operations people) can be bundled with Administration if their function is broad support of the company. They can also be bundled with Engineering (R&D).

In some cases, they can be kept as a separate department called Operations, especially if this is a significant part of the company business. If you are running a factory or data center, then your R&D expense may be minimal, but Operations will be a much bigger expense. In that case, please make Operations a separate line item. *Cost of operations is mostly included in COS rather than as part of*

OPEX *if they relate to variable costs for items sold. But depending on your business (if you have to set up a factory, for instance), Operations can be shown as a separate line item.*

Simply multiplying the total salaries per month by the number of people you employ will give you the cash expense for salaries. (Hint: the Excel SUM-PRODUCT command can do this math quickly.) You should categorize them by departments:

	Annual Salary	1/2010	2/2010	3/2011	4/2010	5/2010	6/2010	7/2010	8/2010	9/2010	10/2010	11/2010	12/2010
Administration													
CEO	$120,000	$10,000	10,000	10,000	10,000	10,000	10,000	10,000	10,000	10,000	10,000	10,000	10,000
Sys Admin	75,000	6,250	6,250	6,250	6,250	6,250	6,250	6,250	6,250	6,250	6,250	6,250	6,250
Admin. Assistant	30,000	2,500	2,500	2,500	2,500	2,500	2,500	2,500	2,500	2,500	2,500	2,500	2,500
COO	120,000								10,000	10,000	10,000	10,000	10,000
CFO	120,000									10,000	10,000	10,000	10,000
Webmaster	75,000							6,250	6,250	6,250	6,250	6,250	6,250
Office Mgr	60,000							5,000	5,000	5,000	5,000	5,000	5,000
Tech Writer	64,000										5,333	5,333	5,333
Tech Support 1	75,000											6,250	6,250
Tech Support 2	75,000											6,250	6,250
Tech Support 3	75,000												6,250
Training Consultant	60,000												5,000
Implementation Consultant	86,000												7,167
Total G&A salaries		18,750	18,750	18,750	18,750	18,750	18,750	30,000	40,000	50,000	55,333	67,833	86,250
Engineering													
VP Engineering	$120,000	$10,000	10,000	10,000	10,000	10,000	10,000	10,000	10,000	10,000	10,000	10,000	10,000
Lead Software engineer	110,000	9,167	9,167	9,167	9,167	9,167	9,167	9,167	9,167	9,167	9,167	9,167	9,167
Developer 1	80,000	6,667	6,667	6,667	6,667	6,667	6,667	6,667	6,667	6,667	6,667	6,667	6,667
Developer 2	80,000		6,667	6,667	6,667	6,667	6,667	6,667	6,667	6,667	6,667	6,667	6,667
Developer 3	80,000		6,667	6,667	6,667	6,667	6,667	6,667	6,667	6,667	6,667	6,667	6,667
Developer 4	80,000		6,667	6,667	6,667	6,667	6,667	6,667	6,667	6,667	6,667	6,667	6,667
Developer 5	80,000			6,667	6,667	6,667	6,667	6,667	6,667	6,667	6,667	6,667	6,667
Developer 6	80,000			6,667	6,667	6,667	6,667	6,667	6,667	6,667	6,667	6,667	6,667
Developer 7	80,000				6,667	6,667	6,667	6,667	6,667	6,667	6,667	6,667	6,667
Developer 8	80,000				6,667	6,667	6,667	6,667	6,667	6,667	6,667	6,667	6,667
Developer 9	80,000								6,667	6,667	6,667	6,667	6,667
QA	75,000					6,250	6,250	6,250	6,250	6,250	6,250	6,250	6,250
QA	75,000						6,250	6,250	6,250	6,250	6,250	6,250	6,250
UI	80,000					6,667	6,667	6,667	6,667	6,667	6,667	6,667	6,667
UI	80,000						6,667	6,667	6,667	6,667	6,667	6,667	6,667
Total R&D salaries		$25,833	$45,833	$59,167	$72,500	$85,417	$96,333	$98,333	$105,000	$105,000	$105,000	$105,000	$105,000
Marketing & Sales													
VP Marketing	120,000	$10,000	10,000	10,000	10,000	10,000	10,000	10,000	10,000	10,000	10,000	10,000	10,000
VP Sales	120,000							10,000	10,000	10,000	10,000	10,000	10,000
Marketing Assistant	46,000										3,833	$3,833	$3,833
Account Exec	80,000											$6,667	$6,667
Product Mgr	90,000							7,500	7,500	7,500	7,500	7,500	7,500
Total S & M salaries		$10,000	$10,000	$10,000	$10,000	$10,000	$10,000	$27,500	$27,500	$27,500	$31,333	$38,000	$38,000

You can itemize salary overhead (items such as employee benefits and payroll taxes) separately, but I suggest adding a percentage to each salary that reflects the overhead on that salary. As I said earlier, I typically use 22-25%. This percentage should also include a portion of the rent, office supplies, and other miscellaneous office-related expenses.

G&A contains all of the expenses that are relevant to the administrative operations of the company but are not directly involved with designing, producing, or marketing a product. G&A will include people such as the CEO, the CFO, the office manager, lawyers, accountants, and any other overhead person that you might think of.

Once these numbers have been added up, you may have some unusual expenses. For example, you may have had to pay some licensing fees or some big trade-show expenses that need to be spelled out separately. Often, most of those things could be in the development department or the marketing department, or they could be broken out in a separate line. That makes up the rest of your expense section.

In the example below I show a detailed model. You don't need to have as much detail in your expense model. You can just make some back-of-the-envelope calculations and use a percentage of the salary number to compute most day-to-day expenses. Just make sure that no big items have been forgotten—for example, sales commissions, affiliate fees and revenue shares, patent fees, technology license fees, leasing fees, shop rental costs, or one-time legal or travel expenses. The model below can be a good check-off reminder to make sure you have included all the big items.

Each business will have its own unique expense categories. Use what is common in your industry. Read some financial statements from other companies, especially public companies. They all have to publish their statements by law, and the statements can be obtained from their websites.

Other Expenses

	Expense Rates by department			1/2010	2/2010	3/2011	4/2010	5/2010	6/2010
	T&E	Supplies	Phone/Fax						
Administration Headcount	$100	$50	$75	2	2	2	2	2	2
Engineering Headcount	$100	$50	$20	4	7	9	11	13	15
Operations Headcount	$250	$50	$20	0	0	0	0	0	0
Marketing & Sales Headcount	$1,000	$250	$200	1	1	1	1	1	1
Total Headcount				7	10	12	14	16	18
Total Salary Expenses				$54,583	$74,583	$87,917	$101,250	$114,167	$127,083

Office Space Costs	Cost/sqft			1/2010	2/2010	3/2011	4/2010	5/2010	6/2010
Minimum space required				1050	1500	1800	2100	2400	2700
Actual space rented				3750	3750	3750	3750	3750	3750
x Rent/sqft	$2.50			$9,375	$9,375	$9,375	$9,375	$9,375	$9,375
+ Deposit				$18,750	$0	$0	$0	$0	$0
+ Utilities at 10% of rent				$938	$938	$938	$938	$938	$938
Office Space Costs				$33,863	$15,563	$15,863	$16,163	$16,463	$16,763

Other Expenses									
Payroll Taxes at 10% of salaries				$5,458.33	$7,458.33	$8,791.67	$10,125.00	$11,416.67	$12,708.33
Health insurance at $750/person				5250	7500	9000	10500	12000	13500
Workers Comp at 0.8% of salary				$436.67	$596.67	$703.33	$810.00	$913.33	$1,016.67
401k at 4% of salary				$2,183.33	$2,983.33	$3,516.67	$4,050.00	$4,566.67	$5,083.33
Travel and Entertainment				$1,600	$1,900	$2,100	$2,300	$2,500	$2,700
Supplies				$550	$700	$800	$900	$1,000	$1,100
Phone/ Fax				$430	$490	$530	$570	$610	$650
Internet				$750	$750	$750	$750	$750	$750
Business Insurance				$4,000					
Legal Fees				$1,000	$1,000	$1,000	$1,000	$1,000	$1,000
Accounting Fees									
Other Organization Expenses				$3,000					
Bank Fees at $5/person				$35	$50	$60	$70	$80	$90
Trade Show									
PC/Furniture at $3000/person				$21,000	$9,000	$6,000	$6,000	$6,000	$6,000
Phone system at $500/person				$3,500	$1,500	$1,000	$1,000	$1,000	$1,000
Development Software at $2000/developer				$2,000	$6,000	$4,000	$4,000	$0	$0
Other Expenses				$51,193	$39,928	$38,252	$42,075	$41,837	$45,598
Total Other Expenses				$85,056	$55,491	$54,114	$58,238	$58,299	$62,361

After you break it down by departments it would look something like this:

G&A salaries	18,750	18,750	18,750	18,750	18,750	18,750	30,000	40,000	50,000	55,333	67,833	86,250
Office related expenses	$51,193	$39,928	$38,252	$42,075	$41,837	$45,598	$63,318	$62,690	$59,650	$67,787	$78,478	$109,429
Rent	$33,863	$15,563	$15,863	$16,163	$16,463	$16,763	$17,363	$17,663	$17,813	$66,675	$39,375	$39,825
G&A expenses	$103,806	$74,241	$72,864	$76,988	$77,049	$81,111	$110,681	$120,353	$127,463	$189,795	$185,687	$235,504
Total R&D salaries	$25,833	$45,833	$59,167	$72,500	$85,417	$98,333	$98,333	$105,000	$105,000	$105,000	$105,000	$105,000
Total S & M salaries	$10,000	$10,000	$10,000	$10,000	$10,000	$10,000	$27,500	$27,500	$27,500	$31,333	$38,000	$38,000

The last three lines are the ones that will be reported with the income statement.

SECTION 3: INCOME & PROFIT

The third section is the EBITDA (which, as you recall, stands for Earnings before Interest, Taxes, Depreciation, and Amortization), also known as net profit. Actually, the word "income" has a legal definition, so using it too loosely can freak out accountants and finance people. That's why I use "Net Profit" or "Net Income from Operations" as a term for the amount I get when I subtract the total expenses from the total gross profits per month or per quarter.

Subtracting the expenses you just calculated from the gross profit will give you the EBITDA. These net profits or earnings give you a good idea of how much money you have left over. Later on, your accountant or CFO can add on taxes, amortization, and depreciation numbers. But depreciation and amortization are non-cash numbers. For the income statement, EBITDA is the main number you will want to have a handle on.

At a later date, an accountant can make this report a GAAP (Generally Accepted Accounting Principles)-compliant income statement. But as an entrepreneur, you don't need to be worried about GAAP compliance at this point. What you really need to do now is make sure you have a rational financial basis for your business. In each industry some commonly accepted ratios indicate how much should be in each category of your report.

A More Accurate Model with Sensitivity Analysis

In many businesses, you don't get paid immediately for your sales. For example, if you ship widgets to your customers, they might not pay you for 30 to 60 days. Therefore, one way to make your report a bit more conservative is to delay revenue collections by 30, 60, or even 90 days to explain your accounts receivable.

When you are getting ready to meet with potential investors, it is a good idea to prepare two to three report scenarios with different assumptions. You must also be prepared to answer the following tricky questions from investors:

1) What happens if your product launch and/or collections are delayed by six months?

2) What if your price assumption is wrong and the price the market will bear is only 50% of what you

assumed? How long will your money last? How will this impact your business?

3) What if your costs are 30% higher? What will be the impact on your business?

4) What will you do if you raise twice (or half) as much money?

I always run these scenarios once I have built the model. This is called "Sensitivity Analysis." Every entrepreneur should do some sensitivity analysis. It is just a good business practice!

Now let's look at an actual completed income statement. I picked one from a publicly traded company called salesforce.com (see the actual page link below). This company sells software products on a monthly subscription basis.

http://www.salesforce.com/assets/pdf/investors/ Q110_Press_Release_w_Financials.pdf

As you can see, even for a large publicly traded company, the format is exactly the same as it is for your startup. Only the size of the numbers will be different. It should not take you more than a day or two to outline various costs and expense items. Then you can create a quick P&L statement that will tell you a lot about your business.

salesforce.com, inc.
Condensed Consolidated Statements of Operations
(in thousands, except per share data)
(Unaudited)

	Three Months Ended April 30,	
	2009	2008
Revenues:		
Subscription and support	$ 281,768	$225,341
Professional services and other	23,156	22,281
Total revenues	304,924	247,622
Cost of revenues (1):		
Subscription and support	37,028	28,710
Professional services and other	24,772	22,588
Total cost of revenues	61,800	51,298
Gross profit	243,124	196,324
Operating expenses (1):		
Research and development	31,584	19,767
Marketing and sales	138,267	122,704
General and administrative	43,150	38,432
Total operating expenses	213,001	180,903
Income from operations	30,123	15,421
Interest, net	4,322	6,722
Other income (expense)	371	(763)
Income before provision for income taxes and noncontrolling interest	34,816	21,380

Conservative or Aggressive?

I believe that you should be conservative while projecting sales and expenses in the early years of your business (i.e., years one and two). As you go into years four and five, it is OK to be bold and make more aggressive assumptions. The investors will judge you on how you perform in the early years of your venture against what you projected. When we look several years out, no one really knows what will happen.

Investors are looking for your enthusiasm and optimism here. An investor will discount your own projections to do their own due diligence, so you should not have to cut numbers in years four and five just to be conservative. The P&L sheet has to look correct as the potential investor looks it over. Otherwise, you will have a lot of explaining to do!

Chapter 6

FINANCIAL RATIOS & SANITY CHECKS

KEY PERFORMANCE INDICATORS (KPI)

There are several indicators, or ratios, that allow readers to quickly gain a deeper level of confidence in your financial model. Examples of these indicators include:

1) Annual revenue per employee

2) Gross margin percentage (How does it compare to other firms in your industry?)

3) Net profit margins (Again, how does yours compare with other companies in your industry segment?)

   Remember, gross profit margin is determined by taking the price per single piece of product and subtracting the cost of goods sold (COGS) expenses. (See Chapter 5, Section 1 for more details on determining gross profit margins.)

   Net profit margin is determined by taking your gross profit margin and subtracting all of the expenses not covered in the COGS. The formula for determining net profit margin is (price − costs)/price=NPM.

4) R&D expense as a percentage of revenue

5) Sales and marketing expense as a percentage of the total revenue

The actual values depend on the industry. You can refer to the annual reports and 10K filings of other public companies in your industry to find out their ratios. If you can get the IPO prospectus, you can get early data from when these companies were starting up. These proxies can go a long way towards establishing credibility with your investors.

WHAT IS TYPICAL?

For a typical software company, G&A expense should be between 8 and 12% of revenue, R&D should be between 12 and 24% of revenue, and sales and marketing will be between 31 and 40% of revenue.

In most instances, investors expect a company to make a profit in years three, four, and five. They will not look too deeply into years one or two, as you are still trying to get started. If the ratios you project for years three to five are not within a range that is typical for your industry, a serious explanation will be required.

My suggestion is that you look to publicly traded companies in your industry and examine their ratios for these departments. These ratios are available on their 10K statements or their annual reports. You can get this information from www.10Kwizard.com or via EDGAR from www.SEC.gov. These numbers will give you a good idea of the ratios for your industry. Your ratios in years four, five, and six should be very close to these numbers. If they are not, then you should ask yourself what is not being counted correctly and what needs to change.

Chapter 7

MORE INFORMATION
THAN YOU NEED!

want to provide some additional thoughts that will help you in creating your business plan.

FINANCIAL CONGRUENCE WITH OTHER STRATEGIES

Tying financial assumptions to other parts of your business plan is an essential check for venture capitalists (VCs). It's easy to see when a team has really worked together to write and develop a business plan. There is nothing worse than reading a business plan and seeing disconnects between various sections.

The following are examples in which this disconnect often appears. VCs have an uncanny way of finding them, even during a 40-minute presentation.

a) Marketing expenses

b) Customer acquisition costs

c) Annual revenue per employee being out of whack for what is normal in your industry ($200K to $400K is normal for software companies). IP companies (IP = Intellectual Property; these companies sell IP or license a model they have created for others to make and sell) can enjoy much higher numbers, while hardware or systems companies may be on the lower side of the scale.

d) R&D expense as a percentage of revenue. Software companies typically have this number around 12-24%, and large, mature companies strive to get their R&D expense to 2% to 4%. If you are a high-flying startup and this number is 4%, it will raise a lot of questions. (These ratios are NOT meaningful in years one and two, since you are not a real company yet. Your focus should be on years three, four, and five.)

e) Talking about international expansion, but showing only numbers for the U.S. market.

As you can see, the numbers do reveal a lot more than you might realize. Please take extra care as you prepare these statements.

FUNDING MILESTONES

As your company grows, it will need financing. The sources of funding change based on the stage you are in. Initially, no one will give you money, except perhaps a parent, until you can show some traction. Bootstrapping means having to fund your own activities on a shoestring. This is when you will end up using your savings or taking out a personal loan. (I cover this subject in much more detail in my new eBook, *Funding Your Startup*, available on www. FiveMountainPress.com.)

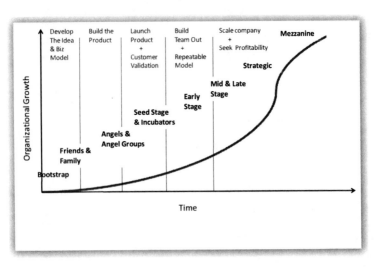

Once you have significant traction, you can approach professional investors who may want to invest in your company. As these sources of funding are completed with venture capitalists (VCs), they are labeled Series A, B, and then C (or beyond). These designations refer to a class of preferred shares issued to these investors in exchange for their money.

Financing names (e.g., Series A, Series C) have special meaning to investors. Indirectly, they indicate the stage a company should be at, and at each stage investors have certain expectations. The chart below indicates what is normal in the industry.

I cover funding in a separate eBook. It addresses:

- How to be investor-ready
- When to approach investors
- Which investors are right for you at what stage of the company
- What investors are looking to see
- How to get their attention
- The process of getting funded
- How to negotiate and what items are most important to you in negotiations

- How to negotiate the term sheet
- All the other funding topics an entrepreneur cares about

SUMMARY

I hope this eBook has been valuable to you in expanding your understanding of what an entrepreneur needs to know in order to run a business. It is by no means a comprehensive book on finance, but it should provide you with a much clearer and better understanding of some of the basic issues with which all entrepreneurs have to deal.

EPILOGUE

I hope that that this book serves as a useful checklist for you as you venture into starting a company or joining a startup. Starting your own business is an exciting, enriching process; you will learn much about yourself. No matter the result, it will be a very rewarding journey.

I plan to write several additional e-books to help you with other questions that will arise—questions about raising money, hiring and recruiting talent, go-to-market strategies, and managing your board and investors. This learning works best when it is shared, so I invite you to write to me and share your stories, advice, and ideas. In this way, others may benefit from your insight and experiences.

Please write to me at naeem@startup-advisor.com

I look forward to meeting you at one of my seminars or clinics very soon.

Naeem Zafar

AUTHOR'S BIO

NAEEM ZAFAR

Naeem Zafar is a member of the faculty of Haas Business School at the University of California, Berkeley, where he teaches Entrepreneurship and Innovation as part of the MBA program. He has also lectured on business, innovation, and entrepreneurship at UCLA, Brown  University, Dalian Technical University in China, and Lahore University of Management Sciences (LUMS).

Naeem is a serial entrepreneur, having started his own business at the age of 26 and gone on to start or work at six other startups. He has extensive experience as a mentor and coach to entrepreneurs and CEOs, and is the founder of Concordia Ventures, a company that educates and advises entrepreneurs and startups on all aspects of starting and running a business.

Naeem most recently served as president and CEO of Pyxis Technology Inc., a company specializing in advanced chip design software for nanometer technology. He has also been president and CEO of two other technology startups, Silicon Design Systems and Veridicom (a Bell Labs spinoff that invented the silicon fingerprint sensors today found on most laptops). Naeem has held senior marketing and engineering positions at several companies, including Quickturn Design Systems, which had an IPO in 1993 and grew to $125M in revenues.

Naeem obtained a Bachelor of Science degree (*magna cum laude*) in electrical engineering from Brown University in Rhode Island, and he also has a master's degree in electrical engineering from the University of Minnesota.

Naeem is a charter member of TiE (The Indus Entrepreneurs, www.TiEsv.org) and a charter member of OPEN (www.OPENSiliconValley.org), where he serves as a member of the executive committee. Naeem also holds several other board positions, including Numetrics Ltd., Brainstorm Pvt. Ltd., and Auxo Inc., and enjoys serving on the advisory boards of several other companies.

Naeem's experience in starting his own businesses, as well as advising hundreds of entrepreneurs and dozens of startups, puts him in a unique position to help others succeed.

To contact Naeem about this book or his mentoring service, email him at naeem@startup-advisor.com.

9 780982 342077